CW00889210

For Walter and Arthur

BLOOMSBURY CHILDREN'S BOOKS
Bloomsbury Publishing Plc
50 Bedford Square, London, WC1B 3DP, UK
29 Earlsfort Terrace, Dublin 2, Ireland

BLOOMSBURY, BLOOMSBURY CHILDREN'S BOOKS and the Diana logo are trademarks of Bloomsbury Publishing Plc

First published in Great Britain 2024 by Bloomsbury Publishing Plc

Consultant vet: Dr Jess French

A catalogue record for this book is available from the British Library

ISBN: PB: 978-1-5266-5743-5; eBook: 978-1-5266-5742-8
2 4 6 8 10 9 7 5 3 1

Printed in China by RR Donnelley, Dongguan City, Guangdong

To find out more about our authors and books visit www.bloomsbury.com and sign up for our newsletters

Do you LOVE PETS?

Matt Robertson

BLOOMSBURY
CHILDREN'S BOOKS
LONDON OXFORD NEW YORK NEW DELHI SYDNEY

Do you love Pets?

**FROM PLAYFUL POOCHES TO MINUSCULE MICE ...
PETS COME IN ALL SHAPES AND SIZES!**

Some of us have cats, some of us have dogs, some of us have rats and some of us have frogs! Some of us don't have a pet at all, but still LOVE everything about them. There's so much to learn about these FASCINATING FRIENDS, or else they might nibble your finger, bite your bum or even POO on your carpet! YUCK!

Pets can be fuzzy or slimy, wet or wild, friendly or shy – but no matter the pet, all they need is LOVE, CARE and RESPECT! So, find a furry, feathered or scaly friend as we cuddle up to discover ...

... what makes PETS so perfectly PAW-SOME!

Get ready to ...

- EXPLORE pet stories from all over the WORLD
- Meet FLYING friends who love to FLAP
- Take a NAP with some expert SNOOZERS
- Dive into the WET WORLD of small SWIMMERS
- Chomp, chew and 'POPCORN' with tiny nibblers
- Create a kingdom for creepies to CRAWL about in
- Grab a lead – it's time for WALKIES
- Remain CALM with some SCALY sidekicks
- Be STAR-STRUCK by some animal SUPERHEROES
- Meet the UNUSUAL companions of the rich and famous
- BE RESPONSIBLE: all pets – big, small or even invisible – need to be cared for PROPERLY!

Pets around

SCOTLAND

In Scotland, it is said that if a stray dog follows you home, it's a sign of good luck – but it's bad luck if it's raining!

FRANCE

In France, some people believe that standing in dog poo is good luck! YUCK!!!

ICELAND

Icelandic horses are the descendants of Viking's horses! They are strong, hardy and pony-sized, which is perfect for Iceland's snowy and icy ground.

UK

In 2012, 12-year-old Emily Hurst started a petition to ban the cruel use of goldfish as fairground prizes. More than 50 UK councils have now banned it!

PERU

Llamas are a huge part of Peru's culture and 25 can be found on its famous Inca site, Machu Picchu. They are gentle and offer great companionship to humans.

the World

GREECE

In Greece and other parts of the world, some people believe that dogs can see ghosts.

Hoooooooowl!

Awooooo!

JAPAN

In Japan, there's an island called Aoshima that has more cats than humans living on it.

MIDDLE EAST

In the Middle East, pigeons are bred to race each other. This dates back to the time of the pharaohs and is continued today. Recently, a racing pigeon was sold for £1,500,000!

AROUND THE WORLD

In parts of the world, black cats are thought to be the pets of witches and people think they bring bad luck. In Wales, it is believed that they can predict the weather! If you hear a black cat sneeze in Italy, you're in for some good luck – ACHOO!

Pets are loved all over the world!

Bird Besties

SQUAWK, CHIRP, TWEET, CHEEP, TWITTER, RING RING!

Humans throughout history have always been fascinated by **feathery, flying wonders**. Some birds chirp joyful songs, whilst others can learn **fun tricks**. There are birds that can even mimic sounds from around the house. These incredible creatures are **full of wonder**, so …

… let's spread our wings and find out more about beautiful birds.

We don't know if pirates really had pet parrots or not – but it's thought the idea was popularised from the book, *Treasure Island*.

SMARTY PANTS

Macaws can copy a huge range of sounds – some even learn to speak!

DOVE-LY FRIENDS

Doves are sweet and gentle. They are very sociable and love interacting with other birds.

SNUGGLE UP

Budgerigars are clever birds that can be very cuddly and love to learn fun tricks.

GREAT ESCAPE

Ring-necked parakeets come from West Africa and India but they're also found in the much chillier UK. It's not clear how they came to the UK in the first place, but one theory is that they escaped from a ship and found freedom on these frosty isles!

A VERY ROYAL PET

King Henry VIII and Queen Victoria both kept African grey parrots as pets. Queen Victoria's was called Coco and could sing 'God Save the Queen'!

PRETTY BIRDY

Cockatiels are small parrots that can copy household noises such as a phone ringing. They also love looking in the mirror.

Listening to birdsong can be good for our mental health. Scientists believe this is because, many years ago, people learnt that if a bird is singing, everything is safe and sound.

DID YOU KNOW? Chickens are closely related to the mighty T. rex.

LOOK OUTSIDE

You don't have to own a pet bird to enjoy these feathery wonders. Next time you go outside, stop for a moment and see how many birds you can see.

Feline Friends

PURRING, FLUFFY LITTLE BALLS OF— WAIT! WHERE HAVE YOU GONE?

It's believed that cats were first domesticated (made tame enough to be kept by humans) at least 9,500 years ago in the Middle East to keep the mouse population down. However, it wasn't until the **ancient Egyptians** came along that cats really became part of the family. For thousands of years, these **fluffy companions** haven't changed that much physically from their wild cat ancestors – although some cats' hunting skills aren't as good as they were, so ...

... let's pounce like a kitten and take a closer look at these purr-fect pets!

American president Abraham Lincoln loved cats and was the first president to bring them into the White House. He would spend hours playing with his cats, Tabby and Dixie.

ANCIENT EGYPTIANS

In ancient Egypt, cats were worshipped as gods and goddesses. If their cat died, Egyptians would shave off their eyebrows out of respect.

OLDEST

Most cats live between 13 and 17 years. However, the oldest cat ever recorded was called Creme Puff and lived to the grand old age of 38!

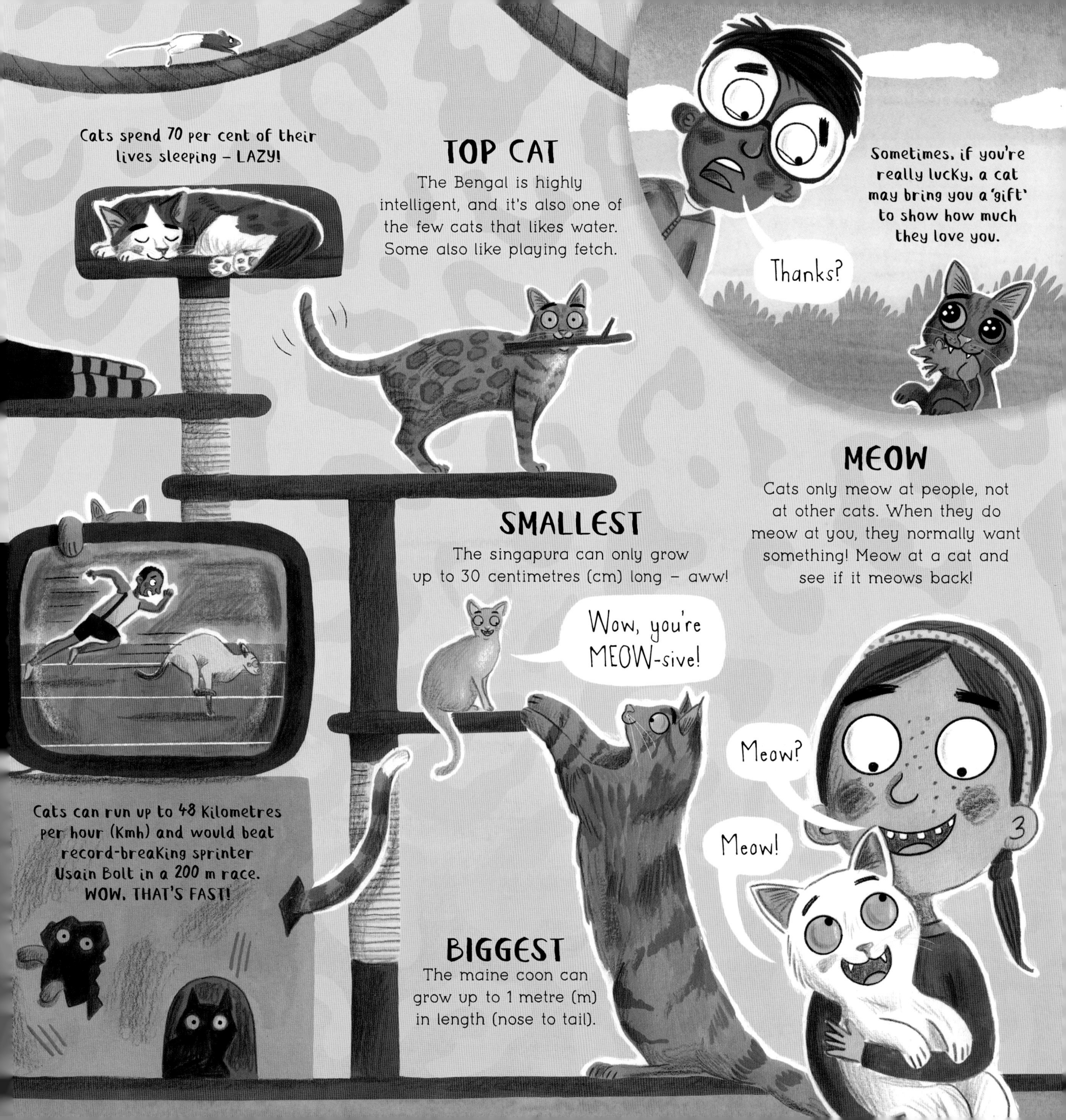
Cats spend 70 per cent of their lives sleeping – LAZY!
TOP CAT
The Bengal is highly intelligent, and it's also one of the few cats that likes water. Some also like playing fetch.
Sometimes, if you're really lucky, a cat may bring you a 'gift' to show how much they love you.
Thanks?
MEOW
Cats only meow at people, not at other cats. When they do meow at you, they normally want something! Meow at a cat and see if it meows back!
SMALLEST
The singapura can only grow up to 30 centimetres (cm) long – aww!
Wow, you're MEOW-sive!
Meow?
Meow!
Cats can run up to 48 kilometres per hour (kmh) and would beat record-breaking sprinter Usain Bolt in a 200 m race. WOW, THAT'S FAST!
BIGGEST
The maine coon can grow up to 1 metre (m) in length (nose to tail).

Splashy Sidekicks

WATERY WORLDS OF WONDER!

Aquatic pets are not only **beautiful** to look at, but it's proven that watching these **fascinating creatures** can be good for you. From coldwater to tropical fish, there are many different species to discover, but remember, different types of **fish** require very different care, so ...

... let's take a relaxing look at these fun fins!

TOP FISH

There are more than 200 types of goldfish. The most popular pet is the common goldfish.

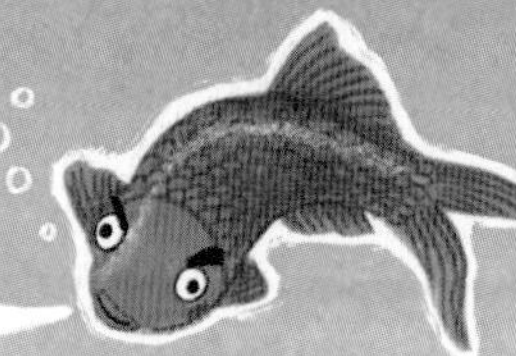

Some fish communicate to each other using a variety of low-pitched sounds and by blowing air bubbles out of their bums – meaning some fish speak FART!

Coldwater Fish

Fish sleep with their eyes open.

EYE SPY

Black moor goldfish have very poor eyesight, despite having bulging bug-like eyes!

LIVING FOSSILS

Sturgeons are often called 'living fossils' because they haven't changed much since the age of the dinosaurs!

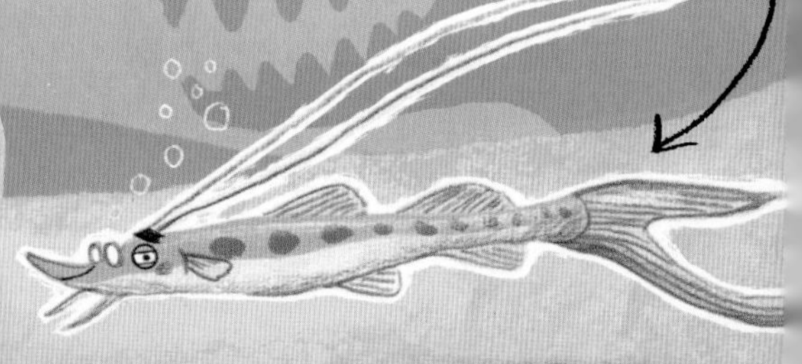

Tropical Fish

GETTING AIR

Dwarf gourami breathe air like humans, so they need to have access to the water's surface.

SEA-MONKEYS

These strange creatures make amazing pets. All they require is a little water and within a few days, you'll have your very own splashy little friends. Don't confuse them with real monkeys though!

GROWTH SPURT

A young zebra danio can regrow parts of its heart!

En garde!

SUPER MUM

Most fish lay eggs, but guppies give birth to live young.

Yipee!

Although fish make lovely pets, most tropical fish should be left in the sea. You should only buy your new fishy companion from a reliable pet shop.

Meow.

WATER WHISKERS

Cory catfish have long, cat-like whiskers. This is what inspired their name! MEOW!

Horseface loach

Chomping Chums

SOME PETS LOVE TO BARK, OTHERS LOVE TO SPLASH, BUT SOME LOVE TO CHOMP!

These little **nibblers** can be the perfect fluffy companions. They don't need walking, don't eat much and take up less space compared to larger animals. Some can **hop**, some can **POPCORN** and they're all super cute. But watch out! Many of them are also nocturnal, which means they are more active (and noisy!) at night, so ...

... grab some earplugs and let's have a sneaky peek at these little squeaks!

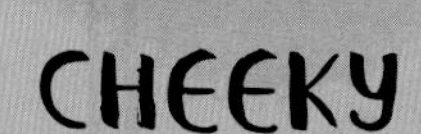

CHEEKY

Hamsters store food in their cheeks to eat later in case food is hard to find. The word hamster comes from the German word *hamstern* which means to 'hoard'.

It's believed that all domesticated hamsters are descendants of two wild hamsters from 1930s Syria.

GNAW

Rodents' teeth never stop growing, so they need to constantly chomp and gnaw otherwise their teeth would become too large.

Chinchillas keep clean by having dust baths.

PLAY FIGHT

Young gerbils playfully box and fight each other – it is a sign that they are happily bonded.

CUDDLE CREW

Chinchillas love to snuggle up to each other when sleeping. In the wild they live in groups called herds or colonies.

FLUFFLES
Rabbits don't like living alone. In the wild they live in large family groups called fluffles.
NEAT AND TIDY
Mice and rats are very clean. Humans often see them as dirty but they groom themselves regularly.
The oldest guinea pig ever recorded lived for almost 15 years! They usually live for 4–8 years.
Yay, it's my birthday!
SUPER SNIFFERS
Rats have an incredible sense of smell. Some rats have been trained to sniff out diseases with more success than microscopes!
SWEET OR SALTY?
When guinea pigs are excited, they jump in the air. This is called POPCORNING!
A group of ferrets is called a business.
HYPNOTIC
Stoats, the wild cousins of ferrets, put their prey in a trance by doing a special dance. Pet ferrets do this too, but it's just for fun!
These pets are little squeak-hearts!

Crawling Companions

NOT SO CREEPY BUT VERY, VERY CRAWLY ...

Can a bug be a pet? **YES**! Bugs make awesome pets. You can watch them go about their **wiggly, buggy** business in their **tiny kingdoms** or see them transform into something completely **new**. Some can **dance**, while others are brilliant at **disguises**! Although some may look a little scary ...

... they could all do with a friend.

MASTER OF DISGUISE

The praying mantis eats other insects and sometimes small birds and lizards. They attack these animals by blending into their surroundings before they strike!

You won't spot me!

DANCE-OFF

Stick insects dance to confuse predators!

Garden snail

EASY EATERS

Snails are one of the cheapest pets to keep as you can feed them kitchen scraps and weeds from the garden.

I'll eat almost anything!

I need a lot of shoes!

MILLIPEDES

These bugs have only three pairs of legs when they hatch but have up to 750 when they are fully grown. Imagine putting on nearly 400 pairs of shoes!

COCOONED

Caterpillars can spend 21 days making their cocoon, and another 14 days inside it to turn into a beautiful butterfly!

TARANTULAS

These spiders shed their outer skin, called an 'exoskeleton'. Young spiders shed every month, and older spiders shed once every year. They also replace organs and can regrow their legs!

SILENT ALARM

In Asia, crickets can be used as burglar alarms! Normally, they chirp away constantly, but if an intruder is nearby, they go quiet. This silence raises the alarm!

ANTS

Ants can carry 50 times their own body weight. This is the equivalent to you picking up a car!

Barking Buddies

SMART, HEAVY, TALL OR SMALL?

Dogs have lived alongside humans for **thousands** of years. From the earliest **hunters** to the handbag pups of **pop stars** today, dogs have always been by our sides. This strong bond makes these adorable animals perfect pets for people all over the world. There are an estimated **500 million** dogs worldwide and there are nearly 200 different breeds, but ...

... which would you take for walkies?

The Border Collie is the smartest dog breed and can learn the name of around 1,000 objects – SMART!

In 1914, an old grave for a man, woman and their dog was uncovered in Bonn, Germany. These bones proved that humans have had pet dogs for at least 14,000 years.

TALLEST

A Great Dane called Zeus stood an amazing 105 cm from the ground – BOW WOW!

SHORTEST

At 10 cm, Miracle Milly the Chihuahua was the smallest dog ever recorded. That is, until her descendant, Pearl, took the record at just over 9 cm!

FASTEST

Greyhounds can reach speeds of 72 kmh. Compared to a Dachshund's 32 kmh, that's pretty speedy!

SENSE OF SMELL

A dog's sense of smell is at least 10,000 times better than ours. They can be trained to sniff out food, money and even diseases in their human pals!

WILD ANCESTORS

All dogs that we see today are related to wolves. It's believed wolves helped early humans with hunting. This bond established the relationship that we still hold today.

HEAVIEST

An English Mastiff called Zorba weighed a massive 155 kilograms (kg) – that's the same weight as two average adult men!

COMMUNICATION

Dogs bark, howl and whine to communicate. In different countries, different words are used to describe this sound. In English we say 'woof' but can you spot the dog 'woofing' in Albanian on this page?*

*The spaniel is 'woofing' in Albanian!

White's tree frog

Cold-blooded Crew

HISS, RIBBIT, SQUEAK ... ROAR!

Reptiles and **amphibians** have been around for **millions** of years, but it is only in the last century that they have made a place for themselves in our homes. Owning your own as a pet has many benefits: they don't **tickle** our allergies, they're cheap to feed and some live a very long time! From frogs to lizards and snakes to tortoises, these **cold-blooded** creatures will soon **warm your heart** with their amazing personalities.

Let's sssssee what we can dissssscover about these sssssssuper creaturesssss ...

RIBBIT!

It is believed that frogs have hopped on the Earth for more than 200 million years.

Red-eyed tree frog

Pacman frog

Amphibians are cold-blooded vertebrates (an animal with a backbone inside its body) that live on land and water.

COLD-BLOODED

Reptiles (including lizards, snakes, turtles, terrapins and tortoises) and amphibians (including frogs, toads and newts) are all cold-blooded. This means their body temperature varies depending on their environment. Warm-blooded animals, like you, maintain a constant body temperature, usually above that of their surroundings.

TWIN TAILS

Some lizards can change colour, some can regrow their tails and others have hairy feet that help them climb.

Your tail!

ESCAPE ARTISTS

Leopard geckos can regrow their tails – this helps them escape predators!

FIVE-A-DAY

Bearded dragons love carrots as a treat and wave to communicate!

Dinosaurs were **HUGE** reptiles – Tyrannosaurus rex actually means 'lizard King'!

INVISIBLE SKILLS

The chameleon is a master of disguise that can change colour to blend into its surroundings!

SLITHERY PALS

Snakes are slithery reptiles with long, thin bodies and no legs. They eat live prey whole and some can be venomous (this means that if they bite you, you can become ill), so always take care around these pets!

H-H-HISS

Colourful corn snakes vibrate their tails when frightened.

Will you be my friend?

SCAREDY-CAT

Ball pythons are shy snakes who can scare easily. But if they're handled from an early age, they can become very friendly.

Snakes can be unpredictable, so always have a grown-up nearby when around them.

SHELL-O THERE!

Tortoises mainly live on land and have large shells on their backs to protect them from predators.

WATER LOVERS

Turtles and terrapins live in water. They have flattened shells to help them swim. Terrapins mainly live in fresh water like rivers or lakes and turtles mainly live in sea water.

GALÁPAGOS GIANT

Harriet the Galápagos tortoise came from the Galápagos Islands in 1835. She spent her final years at Australia Zoo and died aged 176. Most pet tortoises only live between 50 and 100 years!

Extraordinary Pets

SUPER PETS CAN SAVE THE DAY!

Pets are not only **lovable** members of your family, they can also do important jobs in the community. From **guide dogs** to **ferrets**, pets are more than just animals, they are **SUPER** animals! We owe a lot to these incredible creatures, so ...

... let's celebrate the wonders of these extraordinary pets!

CABLE GUYS

Ferrets are sometimes used by electricians to feed wires through tiny holes.

MINIATURE HORSES

These small horses can help children that are having medical treatment because they can be leant on for support.

SUPER PIG

Lulu the pig fetched help after her human had a heart attack. She laid down in the middle of the road so someone had to stop!

CALL ON ME

A cat from America is a hero for learning how to use speed dial! Tommy the cat called an ambulance after his owner fell out of his wheelchair.

FIRE ALARM

Pearly the parakeet raised the alarm when she detected a fire in her owner's home.

CALMING COMPANIONS

Some animals are used in schools. The calming nature of animals such as cats, rabbits, snakes, parrots and guinea pigs are great for helping children with anxiety.

SUPER DOGS

Dogs have been assisting people from all walks of life for hundreds of years.

BRAVE BOY

In 1940, a dog called La Cloche rescued his owner from drowning in the sea. He was the first animal to receive a Blue Cross medal for bravery.

Pet Stars

FAMOUS PETS THAT TOOK THE WORLD BY STORM!

Pets have been companions to many **famous** and **important** people throughout history, from a palace full of 800 pet dogs, to a poet who had a very **unusual** walking companion. Some of these pets became more famous than their owners as stories of these **unbelievable** animals spread across the world.

Let's see what other amazing pets we can discover ...

NOBLE POOCHES

The Maharaja of Junagadh in India had 800 pet dogs and each had their own room, private telephone and butler!

WALKIES

French poet Gérard de Nerval had a pet lobster called Thibault. De Nerval would walk the lobster around the public gardens of Paris.

INTERNET STARS

Some pets have become international stars after appearing on social media sites.

A MUSICAL STARLING

Austrian composer Wolfgang Amadeus Mozart had a pet starling that inspired him to create some of his most famous pieces of music. This amazing bird could even mimic his melodies!

SNAKE EYES

American actor Nicolas Cage once kept two king cobras called Sheba and Moby. He was inspired by their hypnotic, swaying movements, which he mimicked in the film *Ghost Rider*.

BIG CAT

French dancer, World War Two spy and civil rights advocate Josephine Baker had a pet cheetah called Chiquita. They would often be seen walking around the streets of Paris together.

DIVA DOG

The first animal that acted in a movie was a dog called Blair, all the way back in 1905. She was the star of the movie *Rescued by Rover* and after the film's release, the name Rover became a popular dog name.

Perfect Pets

FIND THE RIGHT PET FOR YOU!

Some people prefer small pets, others prefer large pets, some like fluffy ones and others prefer scaly, feathery or even splashy ones. But which pet is right for you?

Let's look through this marvellous menagerie. Can you find your favourite?

Wingspan: 30 cm

Environment: A cool cage and space to fly around

Cost: ££

Life expectancy: 7–15 years

Pros: Sociable and brightly coloured

Cons: Can get sick easily

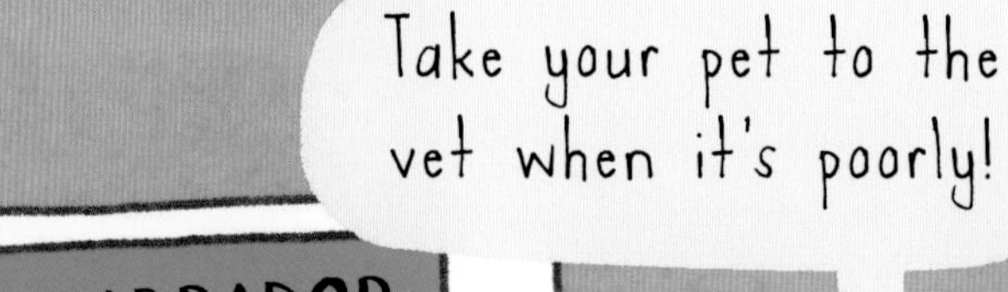

Weight: 5 kg

Environment: Cosy homes where they can curl up and sleep for hours

Cost: ££££

Life expectancy: 13–17 years

Pros: Can be low maintenance and are affectionate purr-machines

Cons: Some people are allergic and litter boxes need regular cleaning

Weight: 30 kg

Environment: Safe homes and somewhere nice to go on walks

Cost: £££££

Life expectancy: 10–12 years

Pros: Will become your best friend

Cons: Require lots of attention, training and walks

Weight: 1 kg

Environment: A quiet home with another rabbit, clean hutch and grass to run around on

Cost: ££££

Life expectancy: 7–10 years

Pros: Can live indoors and outdoors, quiet

Cons: Need plenty of room to roam and are fragile, so take care when you pick them up

Length: Up to 60 cm

Environment: A large tank that can vary in temperature and has low-humidity

Cost: £££

Life expectancy: 10–15 years

Pros: Friendly and chilled, they're also an easy size for handling

Cons: Their tanks need daily cleaning

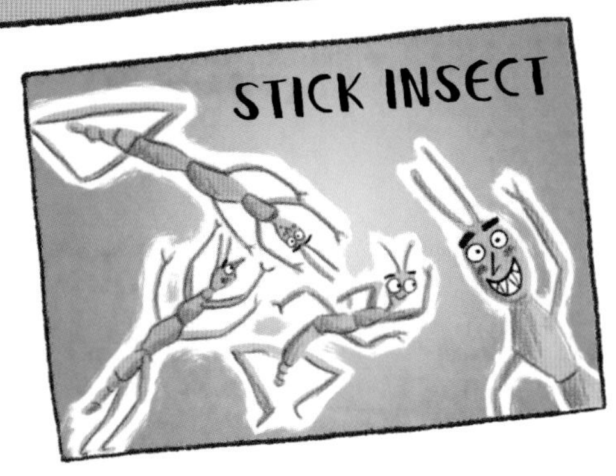

Length: 7.5 cm

Environment: A large, well-ventilated tank with room to climb out of their skins after they have shed them

Cost: £

Life expectancy: 1–1.5 years

Pros: Cheap to feed and allergy-free

Cons: Extremely delicate and shouldn't be handled too much

Length: Up to 7 cm (female)

Environment: Tank with a water heater, filter, rocks and plants

Cost: ££

Life expectancy: 1–3 years

Pros: Low maintenance and very beautiful to look at

Cons: You can't cuddle them!

Size: As long or as short as you would like!

Environment: They can live anywhere in your imaginary world

Cost: FREE

Life expectancy: Can live forever

Pros: Extremely low maintenance

Cons: They can't be seen by anyone else but you

I'm an imaginary pet T. rex called Bob. Who is your imaginary pet?

Explore the rest of the award-winning DO YOU LOVE? series and find out why bugs are **actually** awesome, why dinosaurs are **absolutely** amazing, why exploring is **super** exciting and why oceans are **magnificently** mega! Find these books at all good bookshops and libraries, or visit www.bloomsbury.com

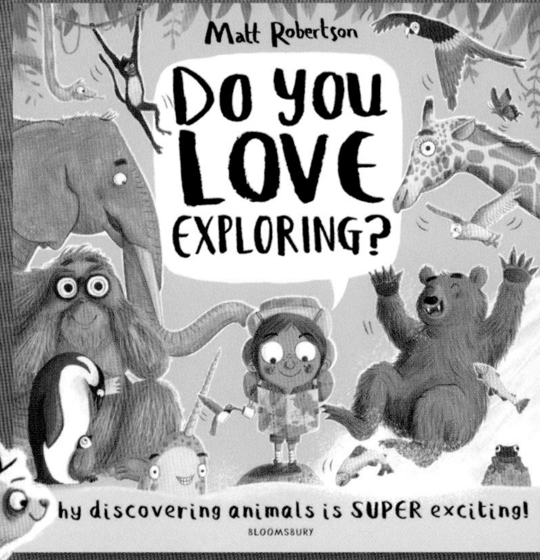

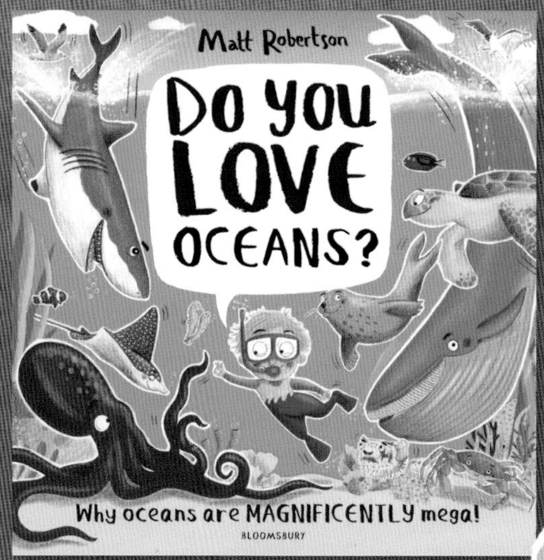

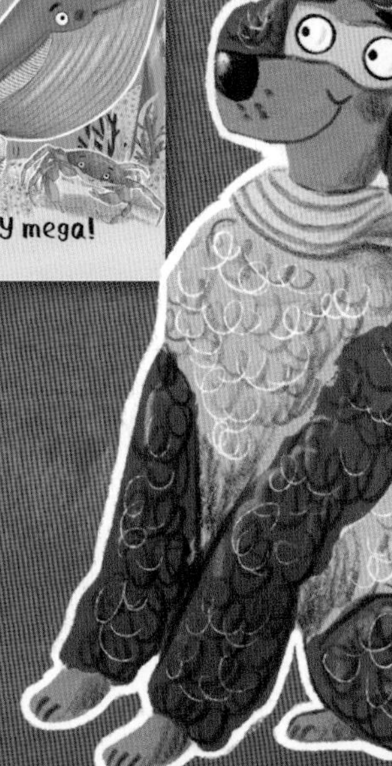